Cooking may be as much a means of
self-expression as any of the arts.
-Fannie Farmer

Chicken Pot Pie

1/2 c. onion, chopped
2 stalks celery, chopped
1/2 c. sliced mushrooms
1/4 c. butter
1/3 c. all-purpose flour
1 t. dried thyme
salt & pepper to taste
2 c. chicken broth

3/4 c. milk
2 potatoes, diced
3 carrots, peeled and
  chopped
1/2 c. frozen peas
1/2 c. frozen corn
2 c. chicken, cooked and
  cubed

Sauté onion, celery and mushrooms in butter in a medium saucepan. Stir in flour, thyme, salt and pepper; add broth and milk. Cook over medium heat until thick and bubbly; set aside. Boil potatoes, carrots, peas and corn in a stockpot of water until crisp-tender; drain. Add vegetables to onion mixture, cook until bubbly; add chicken. Pour into a 2-quart casserole dish and top with pie crust; flute edges. Cut slits to vent, or use mini-cookie cutters to cut out shapes in pastry. Bake at 450 degrees for 15 to 20 minutes. Makes 8 servings.

Pie Crust:

1-1/4 c. all-purpose flour
1/4 t. salt

1/3 c. shortening
3 to 4 T. cold water

Stir together flour and salt; using a pastry blender, cut in shortening until mixture is the size of peas. Sprinkle one to 2 tablespoons cold water into mixture; gently toss with a fork. Repeat, using one tablespoon water at a time until pastry is moistened; roll dough into a 10-inch circle.

Add milk instead of water to pastry dough to give pie crusts a soft golden color.

Chicken & Dumplings

4 lbs. chicken breasts	1/2 t. dried rosemary
2 carrots, thinly sliced	1-1/2 t. dried thyme
2 stalks celery, thinly sliced	2 t. salt
1 onion, chopped	1/2 t. pepper

Place chicken breasts in a large stockpot and cover with water. Add remaining ingredients; bring to a boil. Reduce to a simmer; when chicken is cooked, approximately 30 to 45 minutes or until juices run clear when chicken is pierced, remove from pot, cool slightly and shred. Return shredded chicken to broth and bring to a boil. Drop dumplings by tablespoonfuls on top of chicken mixture; cover and simmer for 20 minutes without lifting lid. Makes 8 servings.

Dumplings:

2 c. all-purpose flour	2 T. fresh parsley, minced
3 t. baking powder	4 T. shortening
1 t. salt	3/4 to 1 c. milk

Combine flour, baking powder, salt and parsley in a bowl. Cut in shortening until mixture resembles coarse meal. Add milk and stir briefly with a fork. If necessary, add additional milk to make dough hold together.

If there's no time to make dumplings, use refrigerated biscuit dough! Cut each biscuit into quarters and drop into simmering stew or soup... just like homemade dumplings.

Velvet Chicken Soup

6 T. butter	3 c. chicken broth
6 T. all-purpose flour	1 c. chicken, cooked
1/2 c. milk	and chopped
1/2 c. whipping cream	1/8 t. pepper

Melt butter in a heavy saucepan; blend in flour until smooth. Gradually stir in milk, cream and chicken broth; cook over medium heat, stirring occasionally, until mixture thickens and comes to a boil. Reduce heat; stir in chicken and pepper. Return soup to boiling; serve immediately. Makes 5 cups.

To season soups and sauces, freeze chicken broth
in ice cube trays and then keep the cubes
in plastic bags in the freezer...so easy!

White Chili

1 lb. dried Great Northern
   beans
4 c. chicken broth
1 clove garlic, minced
1 onion, chopped
4-oz. can chopped green
   chilies

1-1/2 t. chili powder
4 c. chicken, cooked
   and chopped
Garnish: 3 c. shredded
   Monterey Jack cheese

Place beans in a Dutch oven, cover with water and soak over-night; drain. Combine beans, broth, garlic and onion; bring to a boil. Reduce heat; simmer 3 hours. Add chili powder and chicken; simmer one hour longer. Spoon into bowls and garnish with cheese. Makes 8 to 10 servings.

Have some fun with chili toppers! Instead of crackers, try diced tomatoes, sliced jalapeño peppers, a big dollop of sour cream or creamy ranch dressing...don't forget croutons or baked tortilla strips for crunch!

Chicken Cacciatore

4 lbs. chicken, cut into pieces
1/2 c. all-purpose flour
1 t. salt
1 t. pepper
1/2 c. oil
1/4 c. onion, chopped
2 cloves garlic, finely
   chopped
1/2 c. carrots, chopped
1 T. dried parsley
1 bay leaf
1 t. dried basil
4 c. plum tomatoes, chopped
1/4 c. red or white wine

Coat chicken with flour and sprinkle with salt and pepper. Brown in hot oil until golden brown on all sides; drain, leaving drippings in saucepan. Place chicken in a covered dish; set aside and keep warm. Brown onion, garlic, carrots, parsley, bay leaf and basil in oil remaining in saucepan. Add tomatoes to onion mixture; bring to a boil. Add chicken and wine; simmer 30 minutes or until chicken is tender. Makes 4 servings.

Fresh tomatoes from the garden or grocery should always be stored at room temperature to maintain the best flavor. Keep them stem-side down until ready to use so their delicate skin isn't bruised.

Easy Italian Chicken with Pasta

4 skinless, boneless chicken
   breasts
1/4 c. grated Parmesan
   cheese, divided
2 T. Italian seasoning,
   divided

2 T. garlic powder, divided
6-oz. pkg. angel hair pasta,
   cooked
26-oz. jar spaghetti sauce,
   heated

Place chicken breasts in a broiler pan; sprinkle with half of the cheese, Italian seasoning and garlic powder. Broil for 5 to 10 minutes; turn chicken breasts and sprinkle with remaining cheese, Italian seasoning and garlic powder. Broil for an an additional 5 to 10 minutes or until juices run clear when pierced with a fork. Serve chicken over top of pasta and pour sauce over all. Makes 4 servings.

Pasta for dinner? Keep the pot from boiling over by coating the lid with a little vegetable oil first.

Homemade Chicken & Noodles

4 to 5-lb. chicken
3 c. all-purpose flour
1 t. salt
5 eggs

1/2 t. yellow food coloring
white vinegar
chicken broth

Place chicken in a 4-quart saucepan; add enough water to cover. Cook until done, approximately one hour. Reserving broth, remove chicken from saucepan, cool and remove from bone; set aside.

In a large mixing bowl, combine flour and salt; set aside. In a separate mixing bowl, whisk eggs and food coloring together; whisk in 1/2 an eggshell of vinegar. Make a well in the center of the flour mixture; add egg and vinegar mixture. Work dough with hands until all ingredients are completely mixed. On a lightly floured surface knead dough until smooth, adding more flour if dough is sticky. Let dough rest 20 minutes; divide dough in half.

On a lightly floured surface, roll one section of dough into a circle. Continue to roll dough until very thin; cut circle into quarters. Layer quarters on top of one another, flouring well between layers; cut noodles into three long strips, then cut each of the three strips crossways to desired width. Toss with flour to separate noodles; set aside and repeat with remaining dough. Loosely cover noodles with paper towels and let dry one to 2 hours or overnight.

Bring reserved broth to a boil, adding additional canned broth if necessary to equal approximately 2 quarts. Drop noodles into broth, a handful at a time, stirring constantly; reduce heat to a simmer and cook, covered, for 20 minutes, stirring occasionally. Uncover, add reserved chicken and cook for another 20 minutes or until noodles are tender. Continue to stir to prevent sticking. Makes 8 to 10 servings.

Creamy Chicken Casserole

7 or 8 chicken breast halves
16-oz. pkg. round buttery
   crackers, crushed
1/2 c. butter, melted
10-3/4 oz. can cream of
   chicken soup
10-3/4 oz. can cream of
   celery soup
8-oz. can sliced water
   chestnuts
1 onion, chopped
2 c. sour cream

Place chicken in a saucepan; cover with water. Boil until tender
and juices run clear; shred when cool enough to handle.
Combine crackers with melted butter, reserve one cup for
topping. Pat remaining cracker crumbs into a 13"x9" baking
dish. Combine chicken, soups, water chestnuts, onion and sour
cream; spread evenly over crust. Sprinkle reserved crumbs over
top. Cover and bake 30 minutes at 350 degrees; uncover and
bake 5 to 10 minutes longer. Makes 12 servings.

Use hollowed round loaves of pumpernickel bread
to serve up our Homemade Chicken & Noodles.
Bread bowls make a quick and savory meal!

Classics

Crunchy Biscuit Chicken

2 c. skinless, boneless
   chicken breasts, cooked
10-3/4 oz. can cream of
   chicken soup
1 c. canned green beans,
   undrained
1 c. shredded Cheddar
   cheese
1/4 c. canned mushrooms,
   undrained

1/2 c. mayonnaise-type
   salad dressing
1 t. lemon juice
10-oz. tube refrigerated
   flaky biscuits
1 to 2 T. margarine, melted
1/4 c. Cheddar cheese
   croutons, crushed

In a medium saucepan, combine chicken, soup, green beans,
cheese, mushrooms, salad dressing and lemon juice; heat until
hot and bubbly. Pour hot chicken mixture into an ungreased
13"x9" baking dish. Separate biscuit dough into 10 biscuits;
arrange biscuits over chicken mixture. Brush each biscuit with
margarine; sprinkle with croutons. Bake at 375 degrees for
25 to 30 minutes or until golden brown. Makes 4 to
6 servings.

Add freshly snipped herbs such as dill weed, basil or
thyme to biscuit dough for delicious variety.

Picnic Barbecued Chicken Sandwiches

3 lbs. skinless, boneless
   chicken breasts, cooked
   and shredded
1 c. catsup
1-3/4 c. water
1 onion, finely chopped
1 t. salt

1 t. celery seed
1 t. chili powder
1/4 c. brown sugar, packed
1 t. hot pepper sauce
1/4 c. Worcestershire sauce
1/4 c. red wine vinegar
6 Kaiser rolls

Combine all ingredients, except rolls, in a large saucepan;
simmer for one to 1-1/2 hours. Spoon into Kaiser rolls. Makes
6 servings.

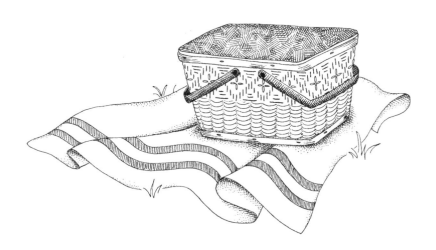

Did you know...a small bunch of mint placed
in the middle of your picnic table or blanket
will keep those pesky bees away?

Hawaiian Chicken Salad

1 c. orzo pasta, cooked
  and drained
1 to 2 skinless, boneless
  chicken breasts, cooked
  and cubed
11-oz. can mandarin
  oranges, drained
1 c. mayonnaise-type salad
  dressing
2 t. sugar
1 t. vinegar
1/4 to 1/2 c. cream or milk
Garnish: slivered almonds,
  toasted coconut and
  pineapple slices

Mix first 3 ingredients together; set aside. Prepare dressing by blending together mayonnaise, sugar, vinegar and enough cream or milk until dressing is of desired consistency. Toss salad with dressing to coat. Place in a serving bowl and sprinkle with almonds and coconut; top with pineapple slices. Serves 4.

Stewing chicken to use later in chicken salads or casseroles? Let it cool in its broth before cutting or shredding...it'll have twice the flavor.

Tangy Citrus Chicken

8 skinless, boneless chicken
    breasts
6-oz. can frozen lemonade,
    thawed
3/4 c. molasses

1 t. dried savory
1/2 t. dry mustard
1/2 t. dried thyme
1/2 t. lemon juice

Place chicken in a 13"x9" baking dish coated with non-stick vegetable spray. In a medium mixing bowl, combine remaining ingredients; mix well. Pour half of the mixture over the chicken. Bake, uncovered, at 350 degrees for 20 minutes. Turn chicken; add remaining sauce. Bake an additional 15 to 20 minutes or until juices run clear when chicken is pierced with a fork. Makes 8 servings.

Clean up's a snap when baking pans are lined
with foil before adding the chicken!

Southern Fried Chicken

1 c. all-purpose flour
2 t. seasoned salt
1 t. baking powder
1/2 t. onion powder
1/4 t. cinnamon
1/2 t. ground ginger

1/2 t. garlic powder
1/4 t. pepper
2-1/2 to 3 lbs. chicken
1 egg, beaten
oil for deep frying

Place dry ingredients in large plastic bag and shake to blend.
Dip chicken pieces in egg, add to bag and toss to coat. Add
enough oil to a large skillet to equal one inch; heat until a drop
of water sizzles when dropped into oil. Fry chicken pieces,
covered, 30 minutes or until tender and juices run clear when
pierced with a fork. Turn chicken every 8 minutes; drain on
paper towels. Serves 4.

Hate cleaning frying pans? Before scrubbing a skillet,
pour in water and about 2 tablespoons of baking soda...
let the pan set and soon, stubborn areas will wipe clean.

Chicken-Tortellini Soup

8 c. chicken broth
1 c. carrots, diced
1 c. celery, chopped
1 onion, diced
2 bay leaves
1 t. dried thyme
2 T. dried parsley

1 t. pepper
1-1/2 c. skinless, boneless
   chicken breasts, cooked
   and diced
1 c. cheese tortellini,
   uncooked

Over low heat, simmer chicken broth, carrots, celery, onion, bay leaves, thyme, parsley and pepper for about one hour or until vegetables are tender. Bring to a gentle boil; add chicken and tortellini. Boil about 5 to 10 minutes, or until tortellini rises to the surface; remove bay leaves before serving. Makes 8 servings.

A toasty touch for soups! Butter bread slices and cut into shapes using mini cookie cutters. Heat on a baking sheet at 425 degrees until crisp and then garnish filled soup bowls before serving.

Vanilla Coffee Mix

1-1/2 c. powdered non-dairy
  creamer
1 c. baking cocoa
1/2 t. nutmeg

1 t. cinnamon
1-1/2 c. sugar
1/2 c. instant coffee granules
2 T. vanilla powder

Combine all ingredients; store in an airtight container.
Attach instructions.

Instructions:

Use 3 tablespoons mix for every one cup boiling water.

Bavarian Mint Coffee Mix

1/3 c. powdered non-dairy
  creamer
1/3 c. sugar
1/3 c. instant coffee

2 T. baking cocoa
5 peppermint candies,
  crushed

Combine ingredients together; store in an airtight container.
Attach instructions.

Instructions:

Use 2 to 2-1/2 teaspoons per cup of boiling water.

Fill an oversized mug with pens, pencils, sticky notes and
Vanilla Coffee Mix. What a clever way to say "congrats"
on landing a new job...makes a great teacher gift too!

Chicken & Vegetable Bake

1/2 c. all-purpose flour
salt and pepper to taste
1 T. paprika
4 skinless, boneless chicken
    breasts
2 T. shortening, melted
1 onion, chopped
1/2 c. carrots, chopped

3-oz. can mushrooms,
    drained
1 T. brown sugar, packed
1/4 t. ground ginger
1/3 c. frozen orange juice
    concentrate, thawed
3/4 c. water
3 to 4 c. rice, cooked

Combine flour, salt, pepper and paprika; set aside 2 tablespoons.
Coat chicken breasts in remaining flour mixture. In a large
saucepan, brown chicken in melted shortening; drain, reserving
drippings in pan. Place chicken in a 2-quart baking dish;
sprinkle with onion, carrots and mushrooms. Blend reserved
flour mixture, brown sugar and ginger together. Add to
drippings; stir to make a smooth paste. Add orange juice
concentrate and water; cook until bubbly. Pour over chicken and
vegetables; cover and bake at 350 degrees for 1-1/2 hours.
Serve over rice. Makes 4 servings.

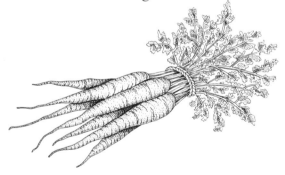

Old-fashioned canning jars in a variety of sizes make
perfect canisters for your country kitchen...
tie a length of homespun around the rim
for a sweet finishing touch.

Lemon-Baked Chicken

1/4 c. olive oil
1/4 c. lemon juice
1 clove garlic, crushed
2-1/2 to 3 lbs. skinless,
    boneless chicken breasts

Garnish: fresh parsley,
    chopped and paprika

Thoroughly mix oil, lemon juice and garlic together; set aside.
Arrange chicken in a 3-quart casserole dish; brush each piece
with lemon mixture. Cover and bake at 350 degrees until
tender; about 45 to 60 minutes. Baste chicken occasionally
with lemon mixture. Uncover for last 20 minutes of baking to
allow chicken to brown. Juices should run clear when chicken
is pierced with a fork. Sprinkle with chopped parsley and
paprika. Serves 4 to 6.

For a quick & easy chicken bake, place boneless chicken
breasts on foil and top with a simple marinade of soy
sauce and sesame oil, Dijon mustard and lemon juice or
even Italian dressing. Wrap foil over chicken and bake at
350 degrees about 20 minutes or until juices run clear
when chicken is pierced with a fork.

Swiss-Mushroom Chicken

3 skinless, boneless chicken
   breasts
3 slices Swiss cheese
1/4 lb. sliced mushrooms
1/2 c. chicken broth

10-3/4 oz. can cream of
   chicken soup
2 c. herbed stuffing mix
1/2 c. butter, melted

Place chicken breasts in a lightly greased 13"x9" baking dish. Add a slice of cheese on top of each breast; layer mushrooms over cheese. Blend broth and soup together; spoon over chicken. Sprinkle stuffing mix on top; drizzle with melted butter. Bake at 350 degrees for 45 to 50 minutes or until juices run clear when chicken is pierced with a fork. Makes 3 servings.

Fresh mushrooms of all kinds are abundant year 'round!
When purchasing them, look for smooth dry caps
without cracks and wash them immediately
before using them but not before.

Sunny Day Chicken Salad

1-oz. pkg. dry ranch
    dressing mix
1/2 c. mayonnaise
1/2 c. plain yogurt
1/4 c. honey
2 c. chicken, cooked
    and cubed
1/2 c. celery, sliced
8-oz. can pineapple chunks,
    drained

8-oz. can sliced water chest-
    nuts, drained
1-1/2 c. red seedless grapes,
    halved
1/2 c. slivered almonds,
    toasted
1 head lettuce, quartered

Mix together dry dressing mix, mayonnaise, yogurt and
honey. Fold in chicken, celery, pineapple, water chestnuts,
grapes and almonds; chill well. Spoon chicken salad in middle
of each lettuce wedge. Makes 4 servings.

Add fresh flavor to store-bought mayonnaise by
adding chopped herbs such as parsley, dill or basil.

Shrimp-Stuffed Chicken

4 skinless, boneless chicken
 breasts
1/4 c. margarine
1/3 c. green onions, sliced
1 lb. sliced mushrooms
3 T. all-purpose flour
salt & pepper to taste
3/4 c. chicken broth

1/3 c. dry white wine
1/2 c. milk
1 c. shredded Swiss cheese,
 divided
1 lb. shrimp, shelled
 and deveined
1/3 c. bread crumbs

Pound chicken breasts until 1/4-inch thick; set aside. Melt margarine in a large skillet over medium heat; sauté onions and mushrooms. Sprinkle with flour, salt and pepper; stir until well mixed. Add chicken broth, wine and milk; simmer over medium heat. Add 1/2 cup of cheese; cook until cheese melts. Remove from heat; set aside. In a small bowl, combine shrimp and bread crumbs; stir in 1/4 cup of sauce, mixing well. Divide into 8 equal portions; place in the center of each chicken breast. Roll meat around stuffing; place seam-side down in a lightly greased 13"x9" baking dish. Pour remaining sauce over chicken; bake at 375 degrees for 20 minutes. Sprinkle top with remaining cheese; bake 5 minutes longer. Serves 8.

Chicken Cordon Bleu

2 eggs
2 c. milk, divided
1 T. dry minced onion
8 slices bread, cubed
and crusts removed
12 thin slices cooked ham

8-oz. pkg. shredded Swiss
cheese
2-1/2 c. chicken, cooked
and cubed
10-3/4 oz. can cream of
chicken soup

Beat eggs and 1-1/2 cups milk together; stir in onion and bread cubes. Place half of the mixture in a 3-1/2 quart slow cooker. Roll individual ham slices and place half over bread mixture. Add cheese and chicken. Combine soup and remaining milk and pour half over chicken. Repeat layers again, topping with remaining soup mixture. Cover and cook on low for 4 to 5 hours or until a thermometer inserted in the bread mixture reads 160 degrees. Makes 8 to 10 servings.

Use a slow cooker for dishes that you would normally cook on the stove. Try stews, chili or even chicken & noodles. It cooks by itself so you have a little more time with family & friends.

Cranberry Chicken

6 skinless, boneless chicken
    breasts
8-oz. bottle French dressing
16-oz. can whole cranberry
    sauce

1-1/2 oz. pkg. dry onion
    soup mix

Arrange chicken breasts in an ungreased 13"x9" baking dish;
spread remaining ingredients over the top. Bake, covered, at
350 degrees for 1/2 hour, basting every 15 minutes; uncover
and bake until done, when juices run clear when pierced with a
fork. Makes 6 servings.

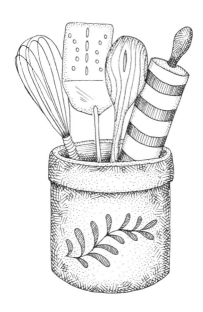

Fill an antique tin with dried cranberries, rosehips and
cloves for a fragrant centerpiece...nestle a votive
in the center for a warm glow.

Maple Roast Chicken & Veggies

1 winter squash, peeled
   and chopped
3 to 4 parsnips, peeled
   and chopped
2 stalks celery, chopped
2 carrots, chopped
1 onion, chopped

1 sweet potato, chopped
6 to 7-lb. chicken
2 T. butter, melted
1/2 t. salt
1/4 t. pepper
1/2 t. dried rosemary
1/2 c. maple syrup

Spread vegetables evenly in a lightly greased roasting pan;
place chicken on top. Brush chicken with butter; sprinkle with
salt, pepper and rosemary. Place on lowest rack in oven; bake
at 400 degrees for 1-1/2 to 2 hours or until juices run clear
when pierced with a fork. Baste about every 10 minutes with
maple syrup and pan juices; remove from oven and let stand
10 minutes before carving. Makes 4 to 6 servings.

To get rid of an onion smell on your hands, simply hold
your hands under cold running water along with a
stainless steel spoon or other utensil.

Chicken-Cornbread Dressing

3-lb. chicken
4 c. water
1/2 c. margarine, melted
1 t. salt, divided
1 t. pepper, divided
6 cubes chicken bouillon
4 c. cornbread, crumbled

1 c. celery, chopped
2 10-oz. tubes refrigerated
    buttermilk biscuits,
    baked and crumbled
1 c. onion, finely chopped
1/2 t. dried sage

Place chicken, water, margarine, 1/2 teaspoon salt,
1/2 teaspoon pepper and bouillon in a large Dutch oven;
cover and simmer on medium heat for one hour or until
chicken is tender. Remove chicken to a platter and let cool;
reserve broth for dressing. Remove meat from chicken and
chop into bite-size pieces. Place in a large bowl and set aside.
In a separate bowl, mix together cornbread, celery, biscuits,
onion, sage, remaining salt and pepper. Slowly add cooled
chicken broth to cornbread mixture until mixture reaches
desired moistness. Add chicken, gently stir and pour into a
greased 13"x9" baking dish. Bake at 325 degrees for
1-1/2 hours. If dressing appears dry during baking, add
extra broth. Makes 8 to 10 servings.

Creamy Chicken à la King

1 c. sliced mushrooms
5 T. butter, divided
1/2 red pepper, diced
3/4 c. frozen peas, thawed
1/4 c. all-purpose flour
32-oz. can chicken broth
3 c. chicken, cooked
   and cubed

1/2 c. carrots, sliced
   and cooked
1 T. fresh parsley, minced
salt & pepper to taste
8-oz. pkg. wide egg noodles,
   cooked

Sauté mushrooms in one tablespoon butter until tender; set
aside. Add pepper and peas to a small saucepan; cover with
water and boil for 2 minutes. Drain and rinse in cold water. In
a separate saucepan, melt remaining butter; slowly whisk in
flour until smooth, cook over medium heat about
2 minutes. Gradually add chicken broth; whisk thoroughly.
Simmer until thick, about 5 minutes; mix in chicken, carrots,
mushrooms, pepper, peas, carrots, parsley and seasonings.
Simmer another 5 minutes, thinning with additional chicken
broth if it becomes too thick. Serve over hot buttered noodles.
Serves 4.

Use tiny terra cotta pots to grow small bunches of
herbs along a kitchen windowsill. It's so easy to snip
fresh herbs for any recipe, or even tie a
festive ribbon around the rim of each pot
to give as gifts to family & friends!

Paprikash Chicken

1/3 c. all-purpose flour
1 t. pepper
1 T. paprika
1/8 t. salt
1 T. dried parsley
6 skinless, boneless chicken
   breasts

1/2 c. oil
1 onion, sliced in rings
2 cubes chicken bouillon
3 c. hot water
1 c. sour cream
Garnish: paprika

Place flour, pepper, paprika, salt and parsley in a gallon-size plastic bag. Rinse chicken; coat in flour mixture. In a large skillet, heat oil and brown each chicken piece; drain, reserving drippings in skillet. Arrange chicken in a 13"x9" baking dish; set aside. Brown onion, bouillon and water in remaining drippings; bring to a boil. Pour half over the chicken; reserve remaining half. Bake, covered, at 350 degrees for 35 minutes; remove and drain. Heat, but do not boil, reserved sauce; stir in sour cream until smooth. Serve chicken over noodles; spoon sauce over top. Garnish with paprika. Makes 6 servings.

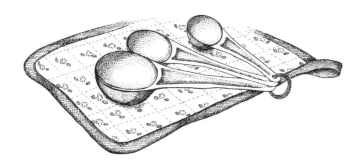

Set a piping hot dish of Paprikash Chicken in a
big basket to take to a neighbor or a sick friend.
Tie on a new set of measuring spoons and
a homespun potholder for a thoughtful gift!

Hot Chicken Salad

3 to 4-lb. chicken, cooked
   and cubed
2 c. celery, sliced
1 c. sliced almonds
1 c. mayonnaise

1 t. lemon juice
salt & pepper to taste
12-oz. pkg. shredded
   Cheddar cheese

Combine first 6 ingredients in an ungreased 13"x9" baking
dish. Top with cheese; bake, uncovered, at 350 degrees for
45 minutes. Makes 6 to 8 servings.

Serve our Hot Chicken Salad on slices of
toasted baguette or half of an herbed bagel.
Garnish with celery sticks and cherry tomatoes
for an extra-special brunch or ladies luncheon.

Shredded Chicken Sandwiches

50-oz. can boned chicken,
   shredded
3 10-3/4 oz. cans cream of
   chicken soup
2 c. fine bread crumbs

1/3 c. dill pickle juice
1/2 sleeve buttery round
   crackers, crushed
40 sandwich buns

Combine first 5 ingredients in a food processor until well
mixed. Heat thoroughly and spoon into buns. Makes about
40 sandwiches.

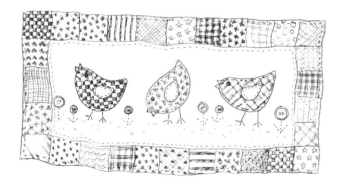

Softened cream cheese is perfect for piping into
cherry tomatoes, pea pods or onto celery sticks...
terrific served alongside sandwiches or salads.

It's easy to keep your pantry stocked using these handy
shopping lists...

Shopping List

Shopping List

Passing along a favorite chicken recipe?
Photocopy our recipe card below, cut out and then just
jot the recipe down...tucked into a card,
it's a delightful surprise!

From the kitchen of :

Index